What's KOOHKA's thing?

Story and Illustration by
Rukmani R.

What's Koohka's thing?

ISBN: 978-93-7062-807-6

Publisher

Books Mantra Publications
(An imprint of Clever Fox Publishing)
www.booksmantra.com

What's KOOHKA's thing?

Story and Illustration by
Rukmani R.

For my beautiful daughter, Vaidehi, whom I love so dearly.

Dear little explorer,

Do your toes tingle when there's something new?

Do your thoughts hop like frogs with nothing to do?

Well, there's someone just like that waiting inside—A jittery-feathery friend with a heart open wide.

He's searching for something, but he's not sure what.

A skip? A swirl? A whoosh? Or a strut?

Will you come along and flap by his side?
His "thing" might be hiding just
one page wide.

With twirls and tickles,

Rukmani

In the deep-dense jungle,
under the big thick oak,
wearing his bright blue crest,
roosted, Koohka, the pea-green
peacock.

Though he had never slept
until after the dawn
but that one morning
he could not get up on his own.

tukk.. tukkk..tuk.. tukk
buzz.. buzzz.. buzz

He was rather woken up by
tuk tukk tukkk on the tree trunk
and rapid buzz buzzz buzzzzz
of the bees working
in a chunk.

...uk..

... buzzzz.. buzzzzzzz buzz.. buzzz.. buzzzzzzz z z

"What are you up to, my friends?"
he asked the bees, rubbing his eyes.
"We are busy making honey. This is our thing,"
they buzzed, swarming in and out of the hive.

"And you, mate Woodpecker?"
he continued asking the bird.
"I am getting my nest ready. This is my thing,"
he chirped, still drilling hard.

“All are skilled, the bees and the bird.
What’s my thing?” Koohka muttered.

So, he took off
with the craze to unravel.
"I will try each and everything out"
he swore, beginning his travel.

After rambling for some time,
he felt a tremor.
Not one but two **giant** rhinos
were battling each other.

"What a combat, sir!"
he stuttered from a distance.
"Could you please teach me the same?"
he took the chance.

"Why not, my pal?" said the rhino.
"Helping a friend is more than just fun.
Just feel the fury inside you,
then go ahead and make a wild run."

Koohka closed his eyes,
"I am ready to shine and slay."
But as the beast charged with boom,
he turned back and dodged away.

Walking a few miles ahead,
he reached a land so dry.
Gliding slowly and majestic,
an eagle was soaring high.

"What a flight, sir!"
he bowed in honour.
"Could you please teach me the same?"
he crowed standing in a corner.

"I would be happy to," said the bird
making a gentle drift.
"Leave your body loose
and jump off the cliff."

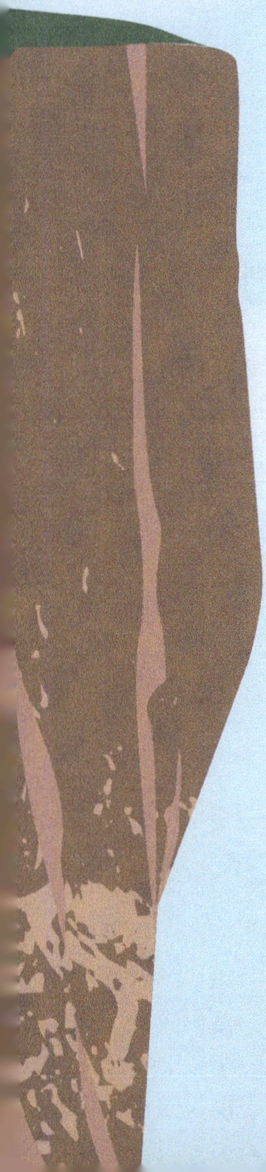

So did he, spread his wings
and took the leap
but instead of soaring high,
he tumbled down the steep.

"Water, I need water,"
he raced to a **huge** pond,
then came a duck waddling,
plump and blonde.

"Now, that's smooth!"
Koohka admired the swimmer.
"Would you be my guru, miss?"
he couldn't help asking her.

"Of course, of course!"
the duck smiled with glee.
"Slowly step into the
pond and follow me."

So did he, gently swept
through the shallow water,
but soon he began to drown
and couldn't paddle any farther.

Roaming in the wild then,
little did he know,
a young cheetah was napping
on a branch, hanging low.

"Excuse me, kiddo!" coughed Koohka.
"I have heard about your speed.
I, too, wish to be as fast as you are.
Kindly do me the deed."

“Sure, why not? You just have to race the wind out,” showed the cub.

But when Koohka dashed after, poor bird just couldn’t keep up.

Then, peeping through the bushes,
he spotted a little brown mole,
smeared with the mud,
he was digging up a hOle.

"What's with the hole, bud?"
Koohka took a stroll around.
"Digging a tunnel to live in,"
said the mole still inside the ground.

"Do you need a hand?"
he wanted to know.
The mole handed him a shovel,
"Here, give it a go."

So did the fowl,
dug and dug the pit,
but as the dusk came by
he had enough of it.

And later at night, when he was
hanging upside down with a bat,
he crashed on his face and frowned,
"I am not even good at that."

He even tried curling up
like a snake in the zoo,
and hopped around as
kangaroos do.

But when nothing worked,
he lost his cheer.
And with a heavy heart,
he wandered off, not knowing
where.

After reaching a land unknown,
hopeless Koohka sat crying,
"What's even my thing?" he wept.
"I am done... I am done trying."

At that very moment as he stood all alone in a street,

the air swayed softly as if dancing on a beat.

Suddenly, he could hear the dum, dum of dhols,
followed by the tooting of flute so sweet and high.
And as he hurried to see where the melody came from,
he ran into a crowd that was standing by.

He tiptoed here, he hopped up there.

But too many heads were in the way.

So up he climbed a giant Sheesham ,

and found a view as clear as day.

Below he saw the fluttering ghagra skirts,
shining like disco lights.
With matkis still over the heads,
the Banjarans danced like lightning strikes.

The bangles tinkled as their
palms moved in gentle arcs.
With each stamping, the anklets jiggled,
and Koohka felt a thousand sparks.

Then he felt a sudden pull he couldn't fight,
his feet just moved, his wings spread wide.
He fluttered down in sheer delight,
and landed softly by their side.

The dancers moved aside with smiling nods,
the crowd leaned in, all eyes on him.
It was then Koohka began to groove,
tapping the floor with a joyful rhythm.

The villagers cheered and whistled,
their eyes grew wide.
"Such grace, such flow.
He moves like a surging tide."

The kids as well shouted "Yay!"
as he hopped around with all his guts.
With steps so sharp, with turns so fast,
his dancing won a million hearts.

Then a dancer came his way,
with pride in her sparkling
eyes.
She gifted him the sacred
jewel.
"This is for you–our dance
survives."

With teary eyes, Koohka bowed

and thanked them all with folded wings.

His heart felt light, his spirit proud.

"I am a dancer- dancing is my thing."

DANCING
WITH THE STARS
Maa, what dance form is it?
This is Lambadi, a traditional folk dance of Banjara community, primarily performed in Telangana, Andhra Pradesh, and Karnataka. It features women in vibrant attire adorned with mirrors, beads, and silver jewelry, dancing to rhythmic beats. The dance celebrates daily life, nature, and seasonal festivities through graceful, earthy movements.

What's KOOHKA's thing?

When the world around him buzzes, dives and charges with purpose, Koohka is left wondering what he's meant to do. He then sets off on a journey through the wild, eager to learn and explore but unable to find his talent, his hope begins to fade. It is when a distant rhythm draws him to the vibrant world of swirling ghagras, jingling anklets and ancient footsteps, that Koohka begins to feel something awaken within.